Iodine!

Thyroid Function

Breast, Prostate, Colon Health

Cancer Prevention

Fibroid Prevention

Brain and Bone Health

Anti-Microbial Agent

Metabolism

Detox

and much more!

A Health Learning Handbook

Beth M. Ley, Ph.D.

BL Publications
Hanover, MN

BL Publications, Hanover, MN 55341
877-BOOKS11
bley@blpublications.com
www.recipesforlifewithdrbeth.com

Knotts, Beth M. Ley 1964-
Iodine!/Beth M. Ley.
p. cm.
"A Health Learning Handbook"
Includes bibliographical references and index.
ISBN: 1-890766-50-X

Printed in the United States of America
First edition, Dec 2016

This book is not intended as medical advice. It's purpose is solely educational. Always consult your medical physician for any medical situation.

Credits:
Typesetting and Cover Design: BL Publications
Proofreading: Jessica Driscoll

YOU NEED TO KNOW...

THE HEALTH MESSAGE

Do you not know that you are God's temple and that God's Spirit dwells in you? If anyone destroys God's temple, God will destroy him, For God's temple is holy and that temple you are. *1 Corinthians 3:16-17*

So, whether you eat or drink, or whatever you do, do all to the glory of God. *1 Corinthians 10:31*

Table of Contents

Introduction

Iodine is a trace mineral that occurs naturally in the environment (53 on periodic table of elements) and is essential to the human body. We mostly depend on food to provide the iodine we need. Research shows that if we don't get enough iodine, it can reduce organ function, and lead to a host of different problems including hypothyroidism, goiter, fatigue, weight gain, mild depression, muscle pain, reduced alertness, dry mouth, dry skin, fibrocystic breasts, ovarian cysts, and even certain types of cancer.

Iodine has numerous physiological functions in the body, way beyond the thyroid. For example, it plays an important role in immune response, digestion, ovarian and breast health.

Iodine also has many topical applications due to it's potent antimicrobial effects. It can be used topically for bacterial, viral and fungal infections, even candida, psoriasis and skin cancer.

Much of the world continues to suffer from iodine deficiency. While many developing countries lack adequate dietary iodine, many western countries suffer from iodine deficiency due to their diets based on processed foods. These foods introduce toxins which disrupt absorption of dietary iodine. This problem does affect women more often than men.

You think you are getting enough iodine from iodized salt? Guess again!

SB (female): I used it topically to heal a bacterial infection on my arm very effectively. I have been taking it internally and experienced a great increase in energy levels.

The WHOLE Body Needs Iodine!

While most people associate thyroid health to iodine levels, iodine actually affects many different areas in the body. Other tissues that absorb and use iodine include:

Breasts
Salivary glands
Pancreas
Cerebral spinal fluid
Skin, hair and nails
Stomach
Brain
Muscles
Thymus
Eyes
Ovaries

Lack of iodine in any of these tissues will lead to dysfunction of that tissue. Hence the following symptoms could provide clues that you're not getting enough iodine in your diet. For example, iodine deficiency in the:

Breasts = fibroids/fibrocystic breast disease

Salivary glands = inability to produce saliva, producing dry mouth

Skin = dry skin and lack of sweating. Hair and nails become dry and brittle. Hair may fall out.

Stomach Mucosa = lack of digestive acid production

Brain = brain fog, reduced alertness and lowered IQ

Muscles = nodules, scar tissue, pain, fibrosis, (fibromyalgia symptoms can develop)

Lacrymal glands of the eye = dry eyes

Ovaries = cysts in the ovaries/PCOS

How Much Iodine Does Your Body Need?

The average dietary intake of iodine for Japanese women is 13.8 milligrams (mg) per day. Some iodine experts, such as Jorge D. Flechas, M.D., M.P.H., recommend 12.5 mg/day, especially for pregnant women to optimize their child's intelligence. Iodine supplementation at higher doses has resulted in children with remarkably advanced intelligence. Other experts advocate much higher doses, as high as 300 mg/day for certain health issues.

Dr. Flechas is the Medical Director of Flechas Family Practice in Hendersonville, N.C. His specialities include Iodine Therapy for thyroid and breast disorders. According to Dr. Flechas, your thyroid alone needs about 6 mg of iodine per day; the breasts of a 110-pound woman will need about 5 mg/day (women with larger breasts need more); and other body tissues, such as your adrenals, thymus, ovaries, hypothalamus, and pituitary gland, need about 2 mg/day.

The earth's soils contain varying amounts of iodine, which in turn affects the iodine content of crops. In some regions of the world, iodine-deficient soils are common, increasing the risk of iodine deficiency among people who consume foods primarily from those areas.

Iodine in food and iodized salt is present in several chemical forms including sodium and potassium salts, inorganic iodine, iodate, and iodide, the reduced form of iodine. Iodine rarely occurs as the element, but rather as a salt; for this reason, it is referred to as iodide and not iodine. Iodide is quickly and almost completely absorbed in the stomach and duodenum. Iodate is reduced in the gastrointestinal tract and absorbed as iodide.

When iodide enters the circulation, the thyroid gland

concentrates it in appropriate amounts for thyroid hormone synthesis. An estimated 70% of the iodine in the body is contained in the thyroid.

Median urinary iodine concentrations of 100–199 mcg/L in children and adults, 150–249 mcg/L in pregnant women and >100 mcg/L in lactating women indicate iodine intakes are adequate. Values lower than 100 mcg/L in children and non-pregnant adults indicate insufficient iodine intake, although iodine deficiency is not classified as severe until levels are below 20 mcg/L.

The current US RDA for iodine is adequate for goiter prevention ***only.***

Pregnancy Exacerbates Iodine Deficiency

Women during pregnancy require higher amounts of iodine to meet their needs, and the needs of the developing fetus. Pregnant women suffering from mild iodine deficiency have been shown to develop more severe deficiencies. If not properly addressed, the thyroid imbalance and hypothyroidism can become a chronic problem even post-partum.

A 2015 swedish study showed the average urinary iodine concentration in the study group was 98 μg/l, which is far less that the recommended minimum levels of 150 μg/l. These low levels may impair the baby's neurological development. (Granfors)

One 1999 study found that thyroid deficiency during pregnancy can lower the child's IQ by about 7 points. The researchers noted that for the first 12 weeks of pregnancy, before the unborn child's thyroid becomes active, the mother is the sole source of thyroid hormones. These hormones play an important role in brain development. Compared with other children, the offspring of thyroid-deficient mothers had impaired school performance and lower scores on tests of attention, language, and visual-motor performance.

Health authorities discovered years ago that iodine deficiency during fetal growth can lead to mental retardation and cretinism. Dietary supplementation with iodine after birth and during childhood does NOT counteract the result of iodine deficiency while in utero. [Hynes] Maintaining appropriate iodine levels during pregnancy, and supplementing when appropriate, is one of the best ways to support proper neural development.

Today we understand much more about iodine and higher levels of iodine supplementation have been used in studies since the early 1900s. High intake of iodine is associated with a lower risk of breast cancer. Low iodine intake is associated with breast, thyroid and liver cancers.[Hassan]

Researchers led by Manal Hassan of Anderson Cancer Center at the University of Texas suggested a clinical association between hypothyroidism and hepatitis C, which is contributing to the rising rate of liver cancer. [Hassan]

Dr. Mark Sircus reported in his book that David Brownstein, M.D., uses between 200 and 300 mgs of iodine daily, with even higher doses for difficult diseases. In perspective, this dose is still far lower than what the 11th edition of the 1910-1911 Encyclopedia Britannica cites as the "usual" doses of 300-900 mgs of iodine daily.

According to Gabriel Cousins, M.D., 6,000 mgs daily of iodine has been used to cure syphilis, skin lesions, and chronic lung disease.

He states, "*The thyroid is only one gland of many glands and tissues that needs iodine. Other glands/organs/systems with high iodine uptake are the breasts, ovaries, cervix, blood, lymph, bones, gastric mucosa, saliva, adrenals, prostate, colon, thymus, lungs, bladder, kidney and skin. Iodine is found and used in every hormonal receptor in the body.*"

Dr. Cousens article "*22 Functions of Iodine*" lists the important functions of iodine:

1. *Iodine helps synthesize thyroid hormones and prevents both hypo- and hyperthyroidism.*
2. *Iodine sufficiency reverses hypo- and hyperthyroidism.*
3. *Iodine supports apoptosis.*
4. *Iodine activates hormone receptors and helps prevent certain forms of cancer.*
5. *Iodine protects ATP function/enhances ATP production.*
6. *Iodine prevents fibrocystic breast disease.*
7. *Iodine decreases insulin needs in diabetics.*
8. *Iodine helps support protein synthesis.*
9. *Iodine deficiency is a global health threat.*
10. *Iodine destroys pathogens, molds, fungi, parasites, malaria.*
11. *Iodine supports immune function.*
12. *Iodine eliminates toxic halogens from the body (including radioactive I-131).*
13. *Iodine regulates estrogen production in the ovaries.*
14. *Iodine is anti-mucolytic (meaning it reduces mucus).*
15. *Iodine neutralizes hydroxyl ions and hydrates the cells.*
16. *Iodine makes us smarter.*
17. *Iodine prevents heart disease.*
18. *Iodine is needed with the use of cellular devices; phones, tablets, smart meters, etc to prevent hypothyroidism.*
19. *Iodine supports pregnancy (as the fetus undergoes more apoptosis than any other developmental stage).*
20. *High doses of iodine may reverse certain diseases.*
21. *High doses of iodine may be used for wounds, bed sores, inflammatory and traumatic pain, and restoration of hair growth when applied topically.*
22. *Iodine helps diminish tissue scarring, cheloids, and Dupuytren's and Peyronie's contractures (hyper-scarring).*

Why Is Iodine Deficiency So Common Today?

The body produces no iodine, it must be supplied through the diet. In some areas of the US, including mountain regions, the Mississippi River Valley, the Ohio River Valley, and the Great Lakes regions, the soil has always had a very low iodine content. But even in other areas of once iodine-rich soil, over farming has frequently depleted the iodine content. Therefore, we no longer get adequate iodine via the plants we consume.

To compensate for this, in the 1920's iodine was added to salt, bread and milk. Today iodine is no longer added to bread or to milk, and the amount of iodine added to salt has decreased. These factors all contribute to the current prevalence of iodine deficiency in the United States.

Iodine Deficiency Symptoms

If your diet lacks iodine, your thyroid gland is usually the first area to be affected. It will enlarge as it tries to increase the production of thyroid hormones. An enlarged thyroid causes a mass in the neck, known as a goiter. As thyroid hormone levels fall, hypothyroidism develops.

Hypothyroidism slows metabolism, causing:

Fatigue
Weight gain
Weakness or pain in muscles
Increased cold sensitivity
Constipation
Dry skin
Depressed mood
Thin and brittle hair and nails

In females, abnormal menstrual cycle
Increased risk for thyroid cancer

Additional non-thyroid related symptoms:

Muscle pain and fibromyalgia symptoms
Dry mouth
Inability to perspire
Achlorhydria (lack of digestive acid production)
Fibroid cysts in breasts or ovaries
Increased estrogen production and an increased sensitivity of the breasts to estrogens (Brownstein)
Polycystic Ovarian Syndrome (PCOS) (Flechas)
Breast Cancer
Candida overgrowth
Psoriasis
Diabetes
Skin infections
Attention-deficit/hyperactivity disorder (ADHD)
Migraine headaches
Swelling and thickening of the skin
Protruding eyes
Decline in mental function

Iodine experts, Drs. Abraham and Brownstein, state that ***over 90% of the US population is iodine deficient.*** *Associated with this increased iodine deficiency is a 690% increase in cretinism, mental retardation, and ADHD in the last several decades.*

The thyroid is only one gland of many glands and tissues that needs iodine. Other areas with high iodine uptake are the breasts, ovaries, cervix, blood, lymph, bones, gastric mucosal, salivary, adrenals, prostate, colon, thymus, lungs, bladder, kidneys and skin. The whole body holds 2,000 mgs iodine, and possibly much more. ***Iodine is found and used in every hormonal receptor in the body.***

Sources of Iodine

Iodine is an important part of our diets, but there are not a large number of foods that provide a significant level of iodine. Here are a few:

1. Baked potato
A baked potato contains around 60 mcg iodine. Make sure to eat the skins because a lot of the nutrients are actually found in the skin and not the flesh.

2. Cranberries
Cranberries are high in iodine, about 400 mcg in 4 oz.

3. Cod
Cod is a good source of iodine. It also contains lots of other nutrients, including calcium, protein and vitamin E, making it perfect for keeping your bones healthy. In a 3 ounce serving you'll get around 100 mcg of iodine.

4. Dried seaweed
Popular in Asian food, dried seaweed such as kelp, nori, kombu, and wakame, is extremely rich in iodine. A small quarter ounce serving may contain 3,000 mcg of iodine. Seaweed is one of the best food sources of iodine, but it is highly variable in its content (see chart below).

5. Boiled eggs
One boiled egg contain about 24 mcg. It also contains protein, vitamins A and D, calcium and antioxidants, making them great for maintaining good health and keeping your cells in good working order.

6. Regular yogurt
Plain yogurt, that has NOT been infused with sugars, will give you 75 mcg iodine in one cup.

Fruits and vegetables contain iodine, but the amount varies depending on the iodine content of the soil, fertilizer use and irrigation practices. This variability affects the iodine content of meat and animal products because it affects the iodine content of foods that the animals consume.

Examples of the Iodine Content Found in Foods:

	Approximate Micrograms (mcg) per serving	***Percent DV****
Seaweed, whole or sheet, 1 g	16 to 2,984	11-1,989%
Cranberries, 4 ounces	400	200%
Cod, baked, 3 ounces	99	66%
Yogurt, plain, low-fat, 1 cup	75	50%
Iodized salt, 1.5 g (1/4 teaspoon)	75	46%
Baked potato, medium	60	40%
Milk, reduced fat, 1 cup	56	37%
Fish sticks, 3 ounces	54	36%
Bread, white, enriched, 2 slices	45	30%
Fruit cocktail in heavy syrup, canned, 1/2 cup	42	28%
Shrimp, 3 ounces	35	23%
Salmon, 4 oz.	32	21%
Ice cream, chocolate, 1/2 cup	30	20%
Macaroni, enriched, boiled, 1 cup	27	18%
Egg, 1 large	24	16%
Tuna, canned in oil, drained, 3 ounces	23	15%
Corn, cream style, canned, 1/2 cup	14	9%
Prunes, dried, 5 prunes	13	9%
Cheese, cheddar, 1 ounce	12	8%
Strawberries	12	8%
Lima beans, mature, boiled, 1/2 cup	8	5%
Apple juice, 1 cup	7	5%
Green peas, frozen, boiled, 1/2 cup	3	2%
Banana, 1 medium	3	2%

**DV = Daily Value. DVs were developed by the U.S. Food and Drug Administration (FDA) to help consumers compare the nutrient contents of products within the context of a total diet. The FDA does not require food labels to list iodine content unless a food has been fortified with this nutrient.*

Iodized Salt

Table salt (sodium chloride) is a processed form of salt which contains sodium and no other minerals.

More than 70 countries, including the United States and Canada, have salt iodization programs where iodine is added. 1.5 grams (1/4 teaspoon) of iodized salt in the United States contains around 75 mcg. iodine. However, today the majority of salt intake in the United States comes from processed foods, but food manufacturers almost always use non-iodized salt in processed foods.

Unfortunately, the process of manufacturing this salt usually includes adding artificial versions of iodine and other chemicals (such as calcium silicate, sodium silico-aluminate and dextrose), making it anything but healthy.

> *In 2008 scientists in Texas found that 53% of iodized salt samples tested contained less than the US FDA recommended level and the level stated on the label.*
>
> (American Chemical Society)

So the real questions are:

1. Do you get enough iodine from your iodized salt?

The purpose of iodization of salt was to prevent goiter and cretinism and not for optimal iodine requirements by the human body. For example, the amount of iodine needed in order to control fibrocystic breast disease is estimated at 50 mgs daily. The amount of iodized salt needed to provide this would be impossible to consume.

2. Does your iodized salt contain any iodine at all?

Many question if iodized salt has any beneficial impact on human health or iodine levels at all. 1.5 grams of iodized salt is thought to contain 75 mcg. iodine. But that measurement is taken at the factory. By the time the salt reaches the grocery store much of the iodine in the sealed container has "vaporized" into the air. Once you get the salt container to your kitchen and open it, more iodine escapes. The longer you keep it, the less iodine remains. Iodine in salt is unstable. In 20 to 40 days an opened container of iodized salt can lose half of its iodine. (Dasgupta)

Sea Salt

Sea salt is the natural form of salt found in the ocean. Sea salt provides approximately 80 different minerals, iodine is one of them. Sea salt provides less iodine than iodized table salt. But what it does contain is in a stable and usable form. Iodized sea salt is also available. The exact amount of iodine in sea salt is unknown as it varies.

Dietary Supplements

Many supplements are available in liquid or tablet/capsule forms containing iodine in the form of potassium iodide or sodium iodide. Supplements of iodine or iodine-containing kelp (seaweed) are also available.

Potassium iodide in liquid form is almost completely (96.4%) absorbed in humans. [Aquaron]

Can seaweed be used to increase iodine intake?

Seaweed sold in the United States has a tremendous variation in the amount of iodine content. In Japan, iodine intake largely comes from seafood and seaweed. However, the seaweed is specifically grown and cultured to maximize iodine trapping. This particular type of seaweed is not readily available in the United States at this time.

When looking for a supplement to get iodine:

You want a product that contains both iodine and iodide. The body needs both forms. Different areas of the body look for one of the specific forms. For example, the breasts need iodine and the thyroid needs iodide.

Also, use a product that provides milligram (Mg) dosages not micrograms (mcg), which are not strong enough to provide the needed benefits, at least for adults.

Goitrogens and Iodine Enemies

Goitrogens are substances that disrupt the production of thyroid hormones by interfering with iodine uptake in the thyroid gland. Certain vegetables, such as broccoli, cauliflower, cabbage and spinach, can block iodine absorption when eaten raw. Others are turnips, mustard, cassava root, soybeans, and the skin of peanuts and millet.

Another is bromide which is commonly added to baked goods such breads, soda pop and sports drinks. etc. Look for "Brominated Vegetable Oil or BVO" on labels and avoid those items.

Prescription drugs that are known to depress thyroid function include lithium bromide, tricyclic and moamine oxidase inhibitors, anti-depressants, dopamine and adenosine. Environmental contaminants include dioxins and PCBs that can also inhibit thyroid function. But the most common is fluoride in tap water and toothpaste.

Halides have a structure similar to iodine and compete for the same receptors in every cell in your body to capture iodine. When exposed to too many of these, your tissues may become iodine deficient:

- **Bromide/bromine** can be found in several forms. Methyl bromide is a pesticide used mainly on strawberries. Brominated vegetable oil (BVO) is added to soda pop sports drinks and citrus drinks. Potassium bromate is found in commercially baked goods and some flours. BVO is banned in food throughout Europe and Japan.

- **Chlorine** (found in tap water, swimming pools, etc.)

- **Fluoride** (found in tap water, toothpaste other dental products, etc.)

Because of the elevated levels of toxic halides in the environment and in the food supply, iodine levels have not only fallen but larger amounts of iodine are necessary to correct iodine deficiency as well as to detox these and heavy metals.

According to renowned iodine expert David Brownstein, M.D. (Board-Certified family physician and Medical Director of the Center for Holistic Medicine in West Bloomfield, MI.) iodine supplementation does not allow these chemical toxins to accumulate in the body. This allows the body to pass these toxins out of the system.

Iodine is the only trace element that can be ingested safely in amounts up to 100,000 times the RDA.

The US RDA for Iodine May Be Severely Insufficient

The current US daily recommended allowance (RDA) for iodine are not in milligram doses but in micrograms. There are 1,000 micrograms in a milligram.

- 150 micrograms (mcg) per day for adults
- 220 mcg for pregnant women
- 290 mcg for lactating/breastfeeding women

However, this RDA was set with the intention to prevent goiter only. Numerous experts make compelling arguments for this intake as completely insufficient for overall physical health and prevention of diseases such as thyroid disease, fibrocystic breasts or ovaries, fibromyalgia and cancer.

The RDA also completely ignores the presence of increasing amounts of goitrogens in the environment.

Toxic halides, including chlorine, fluorine/fluoride, and bromine compete for uptake with iodine in the body, thereby contributing to iodine deficiency.

Iodine is the only trace element that can be ingested safely in amounts up to 100,000 times the RDA.

Iodine Dosages

Everyones needs are different based on their body's ability to utilize the nutrients as well as the level of toxic halide exposure they have each day. If you have a serious health condition then your dosages would be higher than a maintenance dose.

Maintenance: It was once believed that a good daily maintenance dose was between 12.5 and 25 mgs. Today some experts believe this is too low due to our exposure to halides (bromides, fluorides, chlorine, etc.).

Therapeutic purposes such as Cancer: Iodine is absolutely critical for the P53 gene, the "keeper of the genetic code." Without iodine and selenium it will not eliminate abnormal cells from the body such as cancer. Cancer patients take anywhere from 50-300 mgs. iodine daily.

> Michael B. Schachter, M.D. says, *"The treatment dose when a person is iodine insufficient is generally between 12.5 mg and 50 mg daily. Preliminary research indicates that if a person is iodine insufficient, it takes about 3 months to become iodine sufficient while ingesting a dosage of 50 mg of iodine and a year to become iodine sufficient while ingesting a dosage of 12.5 mg of iodine daily. However, the patient needs to be monitored closely with awareness of possible side effects and detox reactions."*

> *"We can only err on the side of too low of a dose. Patients should push their dosages higher and higher until they get the desired result but I recommend doing this slowly unless there is little time as is the case in emergency situations or very late stage cancer. When using a 2% Iodine solution (2.5 mg) one can dose pulse every two hours orally taking each individual dose up to as many as 20 drops and even at this level we are no where near points of iodine toxicity and tolerance. I have given my own 3 year old up to 15 drops in a dose when she was confronted with fever and infection."*
>
> *Dr. Mark Sircus, Ac., OMD, DM (P), Director International Medical Veritas Association, Doctor of Oriental and Pastoral Medicine*

Dr. Brownstein uses much higher doses, between 200 and 300 mgs of iodine daily for his patients, with even higher doses for difficult situations. These doses should only be taken under care of an experienced physician in this area.

Note that these high doses are **not used long term,** only to bring iodine levels to normal. Once a person is sufficient in iodine, the maintenance dose is 12.5 mg daily.

Safety and Side Effects of Iodine Therapy

Iodine Therapy is extremely safe. However, rarely a person could react to very high doses of iodine with hyperthyroid symptoms. High iodine intake can sometimes normalize an overactive thyroid and its symptoms, but if they develop or increase instead, then avoid iodine.

When using iodine over 50 mg daily for a long period of time (more than 3 months), watch for possible overactive thyroid symptoms:

Restlessness — Agitation
Anxiety — Tremors
Weight loss despite an increased appetite
Sweating — Rapid heart rate/pulse
Intolerance to heat — Frequent bowel movements
High blood pressure — Vision disturbances

Thyroid function can be monitored by checking your temperature before getting out of bed in the morning with **Basal Temperature Test.** Measure your temperature by mouth. It will not be inaccurate if you have a sinus infection or cold. Women before menopause measure in the first half of the cycle before ovulation and best in the first week after the start of a new period. The temperature should be 97.6 degrees F or higher, otherwise the thyroid is likely to be under-active. With Iodine Therapy, the temperature will move to normal.

How Do You Know If Your Iodine Levels Are Low?

Iodine testing is not always the best way. Some people like to have a piece of paper that gives definitive test results, sadly these results are often not reliable. I find it works best to treat a person's symptoms and see if that helps. I would treat for an iodine deficiency in people who have markers for iodine deficiency:

- Breast cysts or tenderness, or breast cancer
- Ovarian cysts or PCOS
- CFS, fibromyalgia or unexplained fatigue
- Hypo-thyroid symptoms or thyroid cancer
- Low body temperature of under 98 degrees F.
- Multiple symptoms listed on pages 10 and 11

Iodine deficiency can also be determined with the **IODINE LOADING URINE TEST** but it does require a special lab, most local labs cannot do this test.

This is a good idea for those concidering high doses of iodine (over 25 mg daily) which should not be taken without knowing if there is a need for it.

This test is a laboratory urine test. To do this test, take 50 mg of Iodine/Iodide and then collect your urine for 24 hours. If most of the iodine shows up in your urine (90% or more), that indicates that you have all of the iodine that you need. If less shows up in your urine, then that is an indication that you are deficient state and your body needs more iodine. After Iodine therapy can has begun, a follow-up test can be done in approximately 3 months to monitor progress. Meanwhile symptoms can be monitored.

Places to order the Iodine-Loading Test:

FFP Labs:
Flat Rock, NC 28731
Phone: 877-900-5556 email: ffp_lab@yahoo.com

Doctor's Data, Inc.
St. Charles, IL 60174-2420
Phone: 800 323-2784 http://www.doctorsdata.com

*http://www.**nostudentleftbehind**.org/Iodine.html*

Iodine and Your Health

Due to its important role in fetal and infant development and thyroid hormone production, iodine is a critical nutrient for proper health at all life stages.

Thyroid Health

The thyroid, by far, uses most of the iodine in the body. Iodine is an essential component of the thyroid hormones thyroxine (T4) and triiodothyronine (T3). Thyroid hormones regulate many important biochemical reactions, including protein synthesis and enzymatic activity, and are critical determinants of metabolic activity. They are also required for proper skeletal and central nervous system development in fetuses and infants.

An iodine deficiency can prevent tissues in the body from functioning efficiently, and in turn, stop your thyroid gland from producing two of the hormones it needs: thyroxine (T4) and triiodothyronine (T3). Once this happens, thyroid function deteriorates quickly.

While iodine deficiency is not the only reason behind hypothyroidism, increasing your intake of this mineral can stimulate the hormonal activity that will help you on the road to optimal health.

Thyroid function is primarily regulated by thyroid-stimulating hormone (TSH), also known as thyrotropin. It is secreted by the pituitary gland to control thyroid hormone production and secretion, thereby protecting the body from hypothyroidism and hyperthyroidism. TSH secretion increases thyroidal uptake of iodine and stimulates the synthesis and release of T3 and T4. In the absence of sufficient iodine, TSH levels remain elevated, leading to goiter, an enlargement of the thyroid gland that reflects the body's attempt to trap more iodine from the circulation and produce thyroid hormones.

Thyroid hormones are created not just in your thyroid, but also in a woman's ovaries (thyroid T2), and in the white blood cells of your bone marrow.

Signs of Hypothyroidism:

Slowed metabolism
Fatigue
Weight gain - and inability to lose
Weakness or pain in muscles
Constipation
Dry skin
Depressed mood
Thin and brittle hair and nails
In females, abnormal menstrual cycle/PMS
Increased risk for thyroid cancer
Fluid retention/swelling
Frequent viral infections
Hair loss/thinning
Frequent bruising
Sensitivity to cold/heat
Cold hands and feet
Insomnia
Irritability
Itchiness
Joint aches
Brittle nails
Tingling in hands and feet
Lack of concentration/Brain fog
Depressed immunity
Dizziness
Headaches/migraines
Hoarse voice

According to endocrinologists, more than 40% of the U.S. population is affected on some level by low thyroid function, or hypothyroidism - meaning your thyroid is not making enough thyroid hormones. So if you have a number of the above symptoms, there is a pretty good chance you are.

The frustrating thing for me as a natural health professional is that most of the patients I have who have been diagnosed with hypothyroid, receiving the standard medical treatment of thyroid replacement hormones such as Synthroid, Levothroid, Levoxyl, or Armour Thyroid, is that so many receive no improvement in their symptoms, even though tests show their thyroid hormone levels are now normal. Could it be that treating the symptom (low levels of thyroid hormones) without addressing the most common root of the problem, IODINE DEFICIENCY, is not the best treatment?

Why Is Hypothyroidism More Prevalent in Women than Men?

Hypothyroidism disproportionately affects women at a rate of about 9 to 1 in the US. The reason is that estrogen inhibits the absorption of iodine. Women have higher levels of estrogen.

Hypothyroidism is associated with up to 80-90% free estrogen levels, compared to the normal value of 40-60% free estrogen. Hyperthyroidism is associated with only 20% free estrogen levels, and low iodine intake can lead to a hyperestrogenic state. Estrogen dominance is a common problem today.

Iodine Protects the Thyroid from Radiation

During a nuclear event, radiation in the form of Iodine-131 can be released into the air. Exposure to this radioactive iodine can result in thyroid damage and hypothyroidism. The only way to protect the thyroid is to take iodine (atomic iodine is best) to flood the thyroid with a healthy, stable iodine. This prevents absorption of the radioactive iodine by the thyroid.

Fetal and Infant Development

Iodine sufficiency during pregnancy is extremely important for proper fetal development and yet, still today, it's very common (Lindorfer). During early pregnancy, when fetal thyroid gland development is incomplete, the fetus depends entirely on maternal T4 and therefore, on maternal iodine intake. Production of T4 increases by about 50% during pregnancy requiring an increase in iodine intake. Sufficient iodine intake after birth is also important for proper physical and neurological growth and maturation.

Infants are more sensitive to the effects of iodine deficiency than other age groups, as indicated by changes in their TSH and T4 levels in response to even mild iodine deficiency. To accommodate increased iodine needs during pregnancy and lactation, the iodine RDA are higher for pregnant and lactating women.

Even mild-to-moderate iodine insufficiency during pregnancy may subtly affect fetal development [Hollowell]. In a 2009 study, researchers measured the neuropsychological status of Spanish infants whose mothers received daily supplements of 300 mcg iodine (as potassium iodide) during pregnancy and lactation. [Velasco] The mothers were moderately iodine deficient. Iodine supplementation resulted in significant improvements in some but not all aspects of neurodevelopment (measured by Bayley Psychomotor Development scores) at 3–18 months of age compared with infants whose mothers did not receive iodine.

Breast milk contains iodine, but concentrations vary

based on maternal iodine levels. In a study of 57 healthy lactating women from the Boston area, median breast milk iodine content was 155 mcg/L [Pearce]. Based on reported infant iodine needs and the typical volume of breast milk consumed, the authors calculated that 47% of the women may have been providing their infants breast milk containing insufficient amounts of iodine. During the weaning period, infants not receiving iodine-containing complementary foods may also be at risk of iodine deficiency. [Andersson].

To ensure that adequate amounts of iodine are available for proper fetal and infant development, several national and international groups recommend iodine supplementation during pregnancy, lactation, and early childhood. The WHO recommends iodine supplementation for all women of childbearing age to achieve 150 mcg iodine daily.

For pregnant and lactating women, the recommended iodine intakes are much higher, 250 mcg/day. WHO recommendations for these countries also include breastfeeding through 24 months of age, combined with foods fortified with iodine for children 7–24 months old.

Not all prenatal multivitamins in the United States contain iodine [Leung] and according to 2001–2006 NHANES data, only 15% of lactating women and 20% of non-pregnant and pregnant women in the United States take a supplement containing iodine. [Gregory]

Iodine Deficiency and Autism

According to scientists from the Houston Methodist Neurological Institute and Erasmus Medical Centre, pregnant women who don't make nearly enough thyroid hormone are nearly 4 times more likely to produce autistic children than healthy women. The most common cause of thyroid hormone deficiency is a lack of dietary iodine, because both the thyroid hormones, T3 and T4, contain iodine.

Previous work by Román and others has shown that a deficiency of T4 during a crucial period of embryonic development causes mild to severe brain development errors, such as the lackluster migration of specialized brain cells from the cortex to the outer areas of the cerebrum -- a characteristic of autistic brains.

In a 2007 review Román published in the Journal of the Neurological Sciences, he presented a wide swath of evidence that the near-epidemic rise in autism diagnoses could be at least partly the result of an iodine-starved diet and/or exposure to toxins that interfere with normal thyroid function. (Houston Methodist)

Breasts use a lot of iodine because they are hormonally sensitive and with fatty tissue.

Fibrocystic Breast Disease

Fibrocystic breast disease is characterized by benign lumpy, painful breasts and palpable fibrosis. It commonly affects women of reproductive age, but it can also occur during menopause, especially in women taking estrogens.[Ghent] Breast tissue has a high concentration of iodine, especially during pregnancy and lactation. [Azizi]. Some research suggests that iodine supplementation might be very helpful for fibrocystic breast disease. [Kessler]

Fibrocystic Breasts Linked to Low Iodine

Without adequate iodine, breast tissue is susceptible to estrogenic stimulation. That can lead to the production of microcysts, and those can lead to fibrocystic breast disease. [Lynn] Several animal studies have shown that depriving breast tissue of iodine is an immediate catalyst for fibrocystic breast disease. [Triggiani, Eskin, Krouse]

In a double-blind study, researchers randomly assigned 56 women with fibrocystic breast disease to receive daily supplements of iodine (70 to 90 mcg I2/kg body weight) or placebo for 6 months. At treatment completion, 65% of the women receiving iodine reported decreased pain compared with 33% of women in the placebo group. [Ghent]

Two additional trial showed 70 and 74% of patients improved with iodine therapy, They determined that fibrocystic breast reacts differently to sodium iodide, protein-bound iodide and molecular iodine. Molecular iodine is non-thyrotropic and was the most beneficial form of iodine to use. (Ghent)

A more recent randomized, double-blind, placebo-controlled clinical trial had similar findings. In this study, researchers randomly assigned 111 women with fibrosis and breast pain to receive 0, 1.5, 3 or 6 mg of iodine per day. After 5 months, women receiving the higher doses of 3 or 6

SM (female): I am close to 2 years of taking Iodine. I gradually built up my dosage up to 50-75 mg a day. At one point, I did make it to 75-100 mg a day. Iodine educated doctors often recommend 100 mg a day to reverse Breast Cancer cells and to normalize cells out of balance. I was dealing with very painful fibrocystic breast tissue since a teenager that worsened with natural thyroid support supplements. If we support our thyroid without enough iodine, the body will take iodine from other places to support the thyroid. In my case, the breast tissue, which uses a lot of iodine. My fibrocystic breast tissue has decreased and most months I have no pain. I also have more energy and a much clearer brain for sure! I have read it can take at least 2 years to fully clear the breast tissue. My acne and goiter also improved!

mg iodine had a significant decrease in breast pain, tenderness, and nodularity. The higher the dose, the greater the improvement. There were no major adverse events. [Kessler]

Iodine experts such as Dr. Brownstein have found much higher doses of iodine to be safe and effective for Fibrocystic Breast Disease. He uses between 200 and 300 mgs of iodine daily for his patients, and sometimes higher.

Iodine and Cancer

Iodine actually causes cancer cells to self destruct. Perhaps the absence of iodine in a cell is what causes cancer; statistics tend to support this view.

For example, between 1971 and 2000, the average iodine levels declined by 50% in the US. During that same time, cancers specifically associated with iodine deficiency—such as cancer of the breast, prostate, endometrium, and ovaries—increased.

In Japan, where the average daily iodine intake is around 13.8 mg., they have the lowest incidence of female reproductive organ cancer in their tissues. (Flechas)

Iodine Deficiency and Breast Cancer Linked

Researchers have found that iodine deficiency is a causative factor in breast cancer. Although breast cancer has a number of causes and simply taking an iodine supplement shouldn't be interpreted as a standalone cancer-preventative, studies show a clear correlation between breast cancer and thyroid disorders. [Smyth]

The breasts are one of the most hormonally sensitive tissue. Iodine desensitizes the estrogen receptors, alters the chemical pathways as well as effects the genes, resulting in less cell growth, and causing anti-tumor effect by causing apoptosis (programmed cell death) of malignant cells.

Jonathan Wright, MD has presented evidence that iodide and iodine maintain a proper balance of estrogen metabolism to promote the less estrogenic estriol. (Brownstein)

Bernard Eskin, M.D. reports that rats given iodine will have a variable return to normal breast structure.

Iodine deficiency causes both an increase in estrogen production and an increased sensitivity of the breasts to estrogens. (Brownstein)

Caffeine and chocolate increases fibrocystic changes and fibrocystic breasts have an increased cancer risk. Omega-3's, Vitamins A and E, with other minerals and vitamins, with dietary changes are also recommended.

Treating breast cancer patients without correcting the iodine deficiency can make the breast cancer worse as the thyroid hormone will exacerbate the iodine deficiency.

From the book: *Breast Cancer & Iodine* by Dr. David M. Derry:

> *Iodine could be the first phase of a two phase cancer defense system. It appears that iodine in the extracellular fluid outside of the cells is the main surveillance system for abnormal cells. Iodine also triggers the natural death of normal cells in the body. There are many cells types in the body undergoing a natural death. For example some of the cells in the stomach have lives of only 2-3 days. The name of this process is apoptosis.*
>
> *Carefully documented descriptions of the cancer process at different places in the body reveals most cancers have similar stages through which it passes. The cancers are not really cancer until the cells start to move by invasion through the nearby connective tissue. Cells develop abnormalities for a variety of reasons and can continue to become abnormal all the way up through atypical cells and to carcinoma in situ. Carcinoma in situ is the dividing line between the two phases of cancer*

development. Iodine in correct doses will reverse all of the changes up to and including the carcinoma in situ.

The thyroid hormone controls connective tissue function. So connective tissue around organs forms a structural biological barrier to the spread of cancer. Cancer spread to distant organs only develops in the connective tissue of those organs. Therefore, if the connective tissue defense is not strong then the cancerous cell from a distant site can land there and grow. If, however, the thyroid hormone level in the connective tissue is high enough then the connective tissue will perform its normal defense duties and not allow the cancer cell to enter it and develop.

Using these principles, fibrocystic disease and breast cancer become more understandable. Supplemental iodine in the correct doses will remove all lesions from carcinoma in situ back to just an abnormal cell by triggering death of these cells by apoptosis. Spread of cancer cells in the connective tissue can be arrested by adequate treatment with thyroid hormone to strengthen the connective tissue barrier.

Radiation-Induced Thyroid Cancer

Nuclear accidents can release radioactive iodine into the environment, increasing the risk of thyroid cancer in exposed individuals, especially children. Thyroidal uptake of radioactive iodine is higher in people with iodine deficiency than in people with iodine sufficiency. For this reason, iodine-deficient individuals have a particularly high risk of developing radiation-induced thyroid cancer when exposed to radioactive iodine.

The FDA has approved potassium iodide as a thyroid-blocking agent to reduce the risk of thyroid cancer in radiation emergencies involving the release of radioactive iodine [Center for Drug Evaluation and Research]. The FDA recommends that exposed people take a daily pharmacological dose

(16–130 mg potassium iodide, depending on age) until the risk of significant radiation exposure ends [Center for Drug Evaluation and Research and World Health Organization.

Potassium iodide was widely used in Poland following the 1986 Chernobyl accident and childhood thyroid cancer rates did not increase substantially in subsequent years [Nauman]. In areas where iodide was not used, such as Belarus and Ukraine, many children were mildly iodine-deficient, the incidence of thyroid cancer sharply increased [Center for Drug Evaluation and Research].

Iodine and Parkinson's

Dr. Mark Sircus recommends Iodine (and Magnesium) for Parkinson's. He states in his blog:

"Iodine is found in large quantities in the brain and the ciliary body of the eye. Lack of iodine may be involved in production of Parkinson's disease and glaucoma." Dr. James Howenstein

Long-term iodine deficiency appears linked to abnormalities in the dopaminergic system that include an increased number of dopamine receptors. It is argued that this raises susceptibility to dopamine oxidation which, in turn, causes deficiencies of the antioxidant enzymes, superoxide dismutase, glutathione peroxidase and catalase. Dopamine deficiency also leads to elevated cytotoxic glutamate levels.

The hypothesis that Parkinson's disease may be linked to soil and hence dietary iodine deficiency, associated with glaciation, is not new. In 1987, De Pedro-Cuesta concluded that Parkinsonism had the strongest links with "Early life exposure to a geochemical imbalance, related to the last glaciation, associated to iodine washing out, present in soil, water and diet." (De Pedro-Cuesta)

De Pedro-Cuesta reached this conclusion based on

Parkinson's disease prevalence and mortality in selected age groups and similarities between current levodopa use and goiter distribution, during the period 1920 to 1935. (Foster)

Rat studies indicate that iodine deficiencies can cause reduced brain weight, limited myelin formation, retarded neuronal maturation, a lowering of the production of various enzymes and slowing of the rates of protein and R.N.A. synthesis. Similar processes appear to occur in many neurological diseases.

"In the brain, iodine concentrates in the substantia nigra, an area of the brain that has been associated with Parkinson's disease." David Brownstein M.D.

Recommended dosages are around 50 mg daily, slowly increasing to the optimal amount.

Iodine and Diabetes

Patients with Type 2 Diabetes are at an increased risk of thyroid disease. Thyroid hormones regulate the immune system and metabolism, influence insulin secretion, and cause decreased glucose tolerance.

Reportedly, doctors who prescribe high dose iodine therapy for other diseases such as breast cancer, are finding that iodine can lower insulin and oral anti-diabetic drug requirements in their diabetic patients, and sometimes eliminating it altogether. (Sircus)

Research in Saudi Arabia showed that low iodine levels are associated with insulin resistance in diabetics. They reported that decreased levels of iodine in diabetics likely has deleterious effects on metabolic functions.

The concentration of urine iodine was significantly lower in Type 2 diabetes than in healthy control subjects, Furthermore, they found urinary iodine is negatively correlated with waist, hips, SAD, glucose, insulin, HOMA-IR triglyceride, resistin, angiotensin II (Ang II), and CRP, while it was positively associated with TSH. (Al-Attas)

Another study reported the increased risk for low thyroid and gestational diabetes mellitus in a moderately iodine-deficient area. (Oguz)

An animal study showed the regulation of thyroid function during postnatal development may reduce the precipitation of Type 1 Diabetes. (Hartoft)

A human study showed found that Type 1 Diabetics had larger thyroid volume compared with healthy control groups, and a large portion of them had the markers of autoimmune thyroid disease and iodine deficiency. (Okten)

I could not locate any studies using Iodine Therapy to treat Type 1 or 2 Diabetics, but personally, I think it's a very good idea. Iodine attaches to insulin receptors and improves glucose metabolism, which is good news for people with diabetes. Dr. Guy Abraham (former professor of obstetrics and gynaecology at UCLA Medical School, founder of The Iodine Research Project) recommends up to 100 mg a day for diabetics.

Iodine and Migraines

There are many possible causes of migraine headaches. Low thyroid function and low iodine is one of them.

If you suffer from unexplained migraines and other signs of low thyroid, do the Basal Temperature Test for thyroid function. If your thyroid function tests low (low body temperature), this could be causing you migraines and Iodine Therapy may be your solution. I also recommend magnesium, at least 400 mg daily.

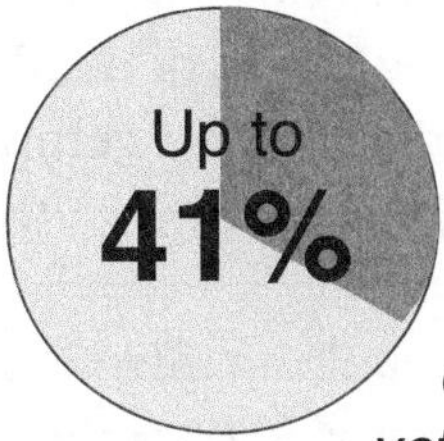

That's your increased risk of hypothyroidism if you suffer from migraines, cluster headaches, tension headaches or other headache disorders. While experts are not sure yet of the connection, they recommend getting tested for an underactive thryoid if you suffer from frequent headaches. (Martin) *All the more reason to give Iodine Therapy a try.*

Chronic Fatigue Syndrome, Unexplained Fatigue or Fibromyalgia

These may also be rooted in an iodine deficiency. Take 6 to 12.5 mg daily for 3 months to see if symptoms improve.

Iodine: Powerful Infection Fighter

Iodine is an excellent antiviral, antibacterial, anti fungal (including candida), mold and yeast agent. It can be used topically or internally. (Arnitz)

Iodine offers a serious and potent replacement for much of the antibiotics that are literally destroying people's lives and can be used safely with children. Parents, who chose not to dose their kids with dangerous vaccines will be glad to know that iodine can be very effective against a host of viral infections.

Not only do some antibiotics increase the risk of sudden cardiac death but sometimes they lead to liver compromise and failure. Despite the ever-widening use of antibiotics the National Center for Infectious Disease and the Centers for Disease Control announced that the U.S. death rate from infectious disease increased by more than 50% between 1980 and 1992, making it the third leading cause of death.

As many as four out of five Americans may be getting antibiotics annually, according to a 2013 study by the Centers for Disease Control and Prevention.

Overuse is one reason antibiotics are making infections harder to treat. Pediatricians prescribe over $500 million worth of antibiotics annually just for one condition, ear infections. Yet topical povidone iodine (PVP-I) is as effective as topical ciprofloxacin, with a superior advantage of having no in vitro drug resistance and reduced cost of treatment.

Women are at risk for vaginal yeast infections (because of the upset of normal bacterial balance) after taking antibiotics. More and more oncologists are seeing yeast and fungal infections as an integral part of cancer and its cause. 40% of all cancers may be caused by infections the subject of antibiotics and the need for something safer, more effective and life serving is imperative. (Kaufman)

Every day, new strains of bacteria, fungi, and other-pathogenic microorganisms are becoming resistant to the antibiotics that once dispatched them.

Though iodine kills 90% of bacteria on the skin within 90 seconds its use as an antibiotic has been largely ignored. Of all antiseptic preparations suitable for direct use on humans and animals and upon tissues, **only iodine is capable of killing all classes of pathogens: gram-positive and gram-negative bacteria, mycobacteria, fungi, yeasts, viruses and protozoa.** Most bacteria are killed within 30 seconds of contact. (Sabracos)

Dr. Derry says that iodine is effective "*for standard pathogens such as Staphylococcus, but also iodine has the broadest range of action, fewest side effects and no development of bacterial resistance.*" There is a world of difference between using an antibiotic – anti-life substance – and an antibiotic, antiviral and antifungal substance like iodine, which is life serving because it is a basic and most necessary nutritional substance.

Iodine kills single celled organisms by combining with the amino acids tyrosine or histidine when they are exposed to the extra-cellular environment. All single cells showing tyrosine on their outer cell membranes are killed instantly by a simple chemical reaction with iodine that denatures proteins. We have natural ways to control pathogens and we should use them and trust them to protect us in ways that antibiotics can't, without the negative side effects.

> ***Iodine is by far the best antibiotic, antiviral and antiseptic of all time. It is the forgotten weapon against Influenza viruses.***
>
> *David Derry, MD, PhD thyroid expert and researcher, based in Victoria, British Columbia*

I even found a journal article discussing Povidone-iodine (the dark yellow one) as an inexpensive, effective topical alternative for managing symptomatic herpes recurrences and other genital tract infections. (Waters) The herpes virus is known to be especially difficult to manage with current treatments such as aciclovir, oral or topical.

Many hospitals use gallons of Povidone iodine daily to help maintain a sterile environment that protects against these harmful organisms. [Tomlinson]

Can Iodine Cure Psoriasis?

Some doctors think so. Tullion Simonicini, M.D., a Roman doctor specializing in oncology, diabetology and in metabolic disorders, discovered that psoriasis is nothing more than a fungus which responds easily and readily to tincture of iodine (7%), due to it's anti-fungal properties.

Iodine tincture is applied topically to the lesions/

scabs several times a day until they soften and fall off with healthy skin underneath. Dr. Simoncini is the author of *Cancer Is A Fungus*, a book where he details his theory and different protocols for different tumor types.

The research of Dr. Simoncini in Rome shows that skin cancers epithileomas, basaliomas, and melanomas are caused by Candida fungus. According to his website, "*Epithileomas, basaliomas, and melanomas cancers have all been successfully treated with an iodine solution of 7%. This destroys the proteins in the fungus completely and works very quickly.*" Dr. Simoncini pioneered sodium bicarbonate (NaHCO3) therapy to treat cancer. For more info visit: www.cancerisafungus.com

Dr. Simoncini also recommends iodine for Candida.

A lack of iodine in the skin manifests as very dry skin and skin that does not sweat when an individual becomes hot.

Dr. Jorge D. Flechas

Candida

Candida yeast overgrowth is central to the causation of many chronic health problems. Researchers at Mayo Clinic have recently made the connection with sinusitis, an inflammatory disease, caused by yeast 96% of the time and cured by anti-fungals, and not antibiotics. (Ponikau)

Candida can localize in specific area - vagina, sinus, anus, or become systemic, where it can be very difficult to get rid of. The treatment protocol to reduce the systemic fungal (yeast) load in a person's body: Potassium Iodide 2%, six to eight drops, four times a day.

For vaginitis, a vaginal rinsing with Povidone iodine can provide rapid relief of symptoms. (Donders)

Iodine Removes Toxins

Dr. Abraham has shown in his work that taking 12.5 mg of iodine promotes the excretion of toxic minerals, such as lead, mercury, and cadmium as well as the toxic halogens fluoride, chlorine and bromide. These toxic halogens are also found in most toothpastes, processed foods and beverages. With Iodine Therapy, these toxins can get stirred up causing some mild symptoms. Patients may experience temporary side effects, such as fatigue and irritability, which can be reduced by lowering the dosage. Also, if you have Candida you could experience a die-off response as the fungus is being killed off. Slow down the amount of iodine if toxic symptoms are intolerable. If you have mucus built up in your body, you may experience a spitting up of mucus. This is a good thing.

A remedy to help reduce detox symptoms is to drink sea salt in lemon water twice daily (12 ounce glass of lemon water with 1 teaspoon sea salt).

Iodine Co-factors

Iodine co-factors help to repair iodine pathways damaged by toxic halides. Vitamin C, Selenium, B Vitamins, (especially B1 and B2), magnesium and manganese.

Iodine/Medication Interactions

Iodine supplements have the potential to interact with several types of medications. Here are a few examples:

Anti-thyroid medications. Taking high doses of iodine with anti-thyroid medications such as methimazole (Tapazole®) can have an additive effect and could cause hypothyroidism.

Angiotensin-converting enzyme (ACE) inhibitors. Angiotensin-converting enzyme (ACE) inhibitors, such as benazepril (Lotensin®), lisinopril (Prinivil® and Zestril®), and fosinopril (Monopril®), are used primarily to treat high blood pressure. Taking potassium iodide with ACE inhibitors can increase the risk of hyperkalemia (elevated blood levels of potassium).

Potassium-sparing diuretics: Such as spironolactone (Aldactone®) and amiloride (Midamor®)

Medications that Interrupt Iodine-Thyroid Function. Medications that use or mimic iodine have been found to interrupt thyroid function. Some drugs like amiodarone can lead to hyperthyroidism (the over-production of thyroid hormones). [Maby-Mottet] Other drugs which can impact thyroid hormone metabolism include interferon, lithium, and dopamine. [Nishikawa]

SAFETY: With elemental iodine (such as Povidone, which is **not** intended for internal use) overdose is possiblem. Symptoms can be abdominal pain, delirium, fever, vomiting, and shortness of breath. More serious symptoms can occur, depending on the way the iodine overdose occurred. If a large amount of concentrated iodine enters the body, it can result in serious damage, When considering working with elemental or concentrated iodine, always know the product and how it should be used.

'Iodine Allergies' - Not Caused by Iodine

While many doctors mistakenly refer to an "iodine allergy," no one has exhibited an allergy to this essential nutrient. Most allergies attributed to iodine result from an allergic response to iodine-based radio-contrast media used to sharpen images from x-rays or CT scans. Studies show the reactions resulted from molecules in the contrast media, not iodine. It is worth noting that while mild symptoms may be the usual response, anaphylactic response and death have occurred. Allergies associated with seafood are reactions to proteins in the seafood, not to iodine.

Iodine for Dogs!

Dogs can suffer from nutritional deficiencies as well. Iodine supports your dog's metabolism and helps them produce thyroid hormones. When iodine levels are too low, hypothyroidism, weight gain, lack of energy, and mood imbalances are common.

In 2002, research showed that after the introduction of iodine in commercial dog foods, thyroid cancer and other tumorous diseases in dogs decreased from 48% in 1982 to 3.2%. (Aupperle)

Although today most commercial dog food does contain iodine as potassium iodide, potassium iodate, sodium iodide, or calcium iodide, it's important to make sure your dog is getting enough. Required intake will vary with your dog's size and age. Without enough iodine, an iodine deficiency can result. Adding a few drops (100 mcg) of potassium iodide to their food one to four times a week (depending on their size and if hypothyroid symptoms are present), should be enough.

Perhaps one of the biggest overlooked nutritional deficiency is iodine!

Almost all of the iodine in the body is used by the thyroid to make the thyroid hormones T-2, T-3 and T-4. At one point in time, there was enough free iodine in our soils and we were able to consume enough iodine through fruits and vegetables. However, due to modern farming practices, most of the iodine and other valuable nutrients are no longer available in our soil. Thyroid and breast cysts can also be from low iodine.

I feel everyone should take 12.5 mgs of iodine daily. Not only to support the thyroid but it is the best antibiotic, antiviral and antiseptic we have! If I eat at a restaurant with questionable food safety, I take 25 mgs!

Fluoride and nitrates are iodine enemies. They compete with each other. Fluoride is a common cause of hypothyroid. People with city water are either drinking fluoride or at the very least, taking showers with it. Also, get rid of fluoride toothpastes!

Thyroid hormone tests do not differentiate between hormones that are bound with fluoride or iodine! When we consume anything with nitrates, iodine is cancelled out. You must read all food packages and eliminate those containing sodium nitrates!

Jeff West, co-author of "Stress Epidemic"

Bibliography

Al-Attas OS1, Al-Daghri NM, et al. Urinary iodine is associated with insulin resistance in subjects with diabetes mellitus type 2. Exp Clin Endocrinol Diabetes. 2012 Nov;120(10):618-22.

Andersson M, Aeberli I, et al. The Swiss Iodized Salt Program Provides Adequate Iodine for School Children and Pregnant Women, but Weaning Infants Not Receiving Iodine-Containing Complementary Foods as well as Their Mothers Are Iodine Deficient. J Clin Endocrinol Metab. 2010 Sep 1.

American Chemical Society. "Iodized Table Salt May Be Low In Iodine, Raising Health Concerns." ScienceDaily. ScienceDaily, 8 February 2008. <www.sciencedaily.com/releases/2008/02/080204090923.htm>.

Aupperle H, Gilesche K, Schoon HA. Tumors of the thyroid gland in dogs–a local characteristic in the area of Leipzig. Dtsch Tierarztl Wochenschr. 2003 April;110(4):154-7.

Arnitz R1,2, Nagl M2, Gottardi W2. Comparison of the Microbicidal activity of monochloramine and iodine. Lett Appl Microbiol. 2015 Dec;61(6):518-22.

Azizi F, Smyth P. Breastfeeding and maternal and infant iodine nutrition. Clin Endocrinol (Oxf). 2009 May;70(5):803-809.

Aquaron R, Delange F, Marchal P, Lognoné V, Ninane L. Bioavailability of seaweed iodine in human beings. Cell Mol Biol (Noisy-le-grand). 2002 Jul;48(5):563-569. [PubMed abstract]

Brownstein D. Iodine: Why You Need It, Why You Can't Live Without It. West Bloomfield, MI: Medical Alternative Press; 2004.

Center for Drug Evaluation and Research, Food and Drug Administration. Guidance. Potassium iodide as a thyroid blocking agent in radiation emergenciesexternal link disclaimer. December 2001.

Dasgupta PK(1), Liu Y, Dyke JV. Environ Sci Technol. Iodine nutrition: iodine content of iodized salt in the United States. 2008 Feb 15;42(4):1315-23.

de Benoist B, McLean E, Andersson M, Rogers L. Iodine deficiency in 2007: global progress since 2003. Food Nutr Bull. 2008;29:195-202.

De Pedro-Cuesta J. Studies on the prevalence of Paralysis Agitans by tracer methodology. Acta Neurol Scand, 1987. Suppl 112, 75: 106

Donders GG1, Ruban K, Bellen G. Selecting anti-microbial treatment of aerobic vaginitis. Curr Infect Dis Rep. 2015 May;17(5):477.

Derry D. Iodine: the Forgotten Weapon Against Influenza Viruses.Thyroid Science 4(9):R1-5, 2009

Eskin BA. Iodine and mammary cancer. Adv Exp Med Biol. 1977;91:293-304.

Farrow, L, The Iodine Crisis, Devon Press, 2013,

Foster, H., Parkinson's Disease, Multiple Sclerosis and Amyotrophic Lateral Sclerosis: The Iodine-Dopachrome-Glutamate Hypothesis. The Journal of Orthomolecular Medicine Vol. 14, 3rd Quarter 1999

Ghent WR, Eskin BA, Low DA, Hill LP. Iodine replacement in fibrocystic disease of the breast. Can J Surg. 1993 Oct;36(5):453-460.

Granfors, M, Andersson, M et al. Iodine deficiency in a study population of pregnant women in Sweden. Acta Obstetricia et Gynecologica Scandinavica, 2015; DOI: 10.1111/aogs.12713

Gregory CO, Serdula MK, Sullivan KM. Use of supplements with and without iodine in women of childbearing age in the United States. Thyroid. 2009 Sep;19(9):1019-1020.

Hartoft-Nielsen ML, Rasmussen AK, et al. Iodine and tri-iodo-thyronine reduce the incidence of type 1 diabetes mellitus in the autoimmune prone BB rats. Autoimmunity. 2009 Feb;42(2):131-8.

Hassan, Manal et al; Association Between Hypothyroidism and Hepatocellular Carcinoma: USA Case-Control Study. Hepatology, May 2009

Hollowell JG, Haddow JE. The prevalence of iodine deficiency in women of reproductive age in the United States of America. Public Health Nutr. 2007 Dec;10(12A):1532-1539; discussion 1540-1541.

Houston Methodist. "Autism four times likelier when mother's thyroid is weakened." ScienceDaily. ScienceDaily, 13 August 2013. <www.sciencedaily.com/releases/2013/08/130813111730.htm>.

Hynes KL, Otahal P, Hay I, Burgess JR. Mild iodine deficiency during pregnancy is associated with reduced educational outcomes in the offspring: 9-year follow-up of the gestational iodine cohort. J Clin Endocrinol Metab. 2013 May;98(5):1954-62. doi: 10.1210/jc.2012-4249. Epub 2013 Apr 30.

Kessler JH. The effect of supraphysiologic levels of iodine on patients with cyclic mastalgia. Breast J. 2004 Jul-Aug;10(4):328-336.

Krouse TB, Eskin BA, Mobini J. Age-related changes resembling fibrocystic disease in iodine-blocked rat breasts. Arch Pathol Lab Med. 1979 Nov;103(12):631-4.

Leung AM, Pearce EN, Braverman LE. Iodine content of prenatal multivitamins in the United States. N Engl J Med. 2009 Feb 26;360(9):939-940.

Lindorfer, H, Krebs, Kautzky-Willer, et. al. Iodine deficiency in pregnant women in Austria. European Journal of Clinical Nutrition, 2014; DOI: 10.1038/ejcn.2014.253

Lynn C. Hartmann, M.D., Thomas A. Sellers, Ph.D., et al. Benign Breast Disease and the Risk of Breast Cancer. N Engl J Med 2005; 353:229-237July 21, 2005

Maby-Mottet V, Ollo D, Meyer P. [Amiodarone and thyroid]. Rev Med Suisse. 2012 Nov 14;8(362):2175-6, 2178-80.

Martin, A, Pinney, S et al, Headache Disorders May Be a Risk Factor for the Development of New Onset Hypothyroidism. Headache, 27 September 2016, DOI: 10.1111/head.12943.

Nauman J, Wolff J. Iodide prophylaxis in Poland after the Chernobyl reactor accident: benefits and risks. Am J Med 1993;94:524-532.

Nishikawa M, Toyoda N, Nomura E. [Drug-induced thyroid dysfunction]. Nihon Rinsho. 2012 Nov;70(11):1958-64.

Oguz A, Tuzun D, et al. Frequency of isolated maternal hypothyroxinemia in women with gestational diabetes mellitus in a moderately iodine-deficient area. Gynecol Endocrinol. 2015 Oct;31(10):792-5.

Oguz A, Tuzun D, et al. Prevalance of gestational diabetes mellitus in patients with gestational transient thyrotoxicosis. Gynecol Endocrinol. 2013 Apr;29(4):336-9.

Okten A1, Akcay S. et al. Iodine status, thyroid function, thyroid volume and thyroid autoimmunity in patients with type 1 diabetes mellitus in an iodine-replete area. Diabetes Metab. 2006 Sep;32(4):323-9.

Pearce EN, Leung AM, Blount BC, et al Breast milk iodine and perchlorate concentrations in lactating Boston-area women. J Clin Endocrinol Metab. 2007 May;92(5):1673-1677.

Ponikau JU1, Sherris DA, Kern EB, et al. The diagnosis and incidence of allergic fungal sinusitis. Mayo Clin Proc. 1999 Sep;74(9):877-84.

Sabracos L.,Romanou S., et al. The in vitro effective antiviral action of povidone–iodine (PVP–I) may also have therapeutic potential by its intravenous administration diluted with Ringer's solution. Med Hyp. Volume 68, Issue 2, 2007, Pages 272–274

Sircus M. http://drsircus.com/medicine/parkinsons-disease/#_edn10

Smyth PP. The thyroid, iodine and breast cancer. Breast Cancer Research : BCR. 2003;5(5):235-238.

Tomlinson M, Adams V, Chopra M, Jooste P, et al. Survey of iodine deficiency and intestinal parasitic infections in school-going children: Bie Province, Angola. Public Health Nutr. 2010 Sep; 13(9): 1314-8.

Triggiani V, Tafaro E, Giagulli VA, et al. Role of iodine, selenium and other micronutrients in thyroid function and disorders. Endocr Metab Immune Disord Drug Targets. 2009 Sep;9(3):277-94.

Velasco I, Carreira M, Santiago P, et al Effect of iodine prophylaxis during pregnancy on neurocognitive development of children during the first two years of life. J Clin Endocrinol Metab. 2009 Sep;94(9):3234-3241

Warren HV: Geology and multiple sclerosis. Nature, 1959, 184: 56

Waters, L. J.; Barton, S. E.; Boag, F. C. Betadine for herpes simplex infection. International Journal of STD & AIDS;Dec2006, Vol. 17 Issue 12, p854

World Health Organization. Guidelines for Iodine Prophylaxis following Nuclear Accidentsexternal link disclaimer. 1999.

Zimmermann MB. Iodine deficiency in pregnancy and the effects of maternal iodine supplementation on the offspring: a review. Am J Clin Nutr. 2009 Feb;89(2):668S-672S.

About The Author...

Beth M. Ley, Ph.D., has been a science writer specializing in health and nutrition since 1988 and has written many health-related books, including the best sellers, ***DHEA: Unlocking the Secrets to the Fountain of Youth*** and ***MSM: On Our Way Back to Health With Sulfur***. She wrote her own undergraduate degree program and graduated in Scientific and Technical Writing from North Dakota State University in 1987 (combination of Zoology and Journalism). Dr. Beth has her masters (1998) and doctoral degrees (1999) in Nutrition.

Dr. Beth does Biblical-based nutrition and wellness counseling on line (www.recipesforlifewithdrbeth.com). She speaks on Biblical nutrition, health and Divine healing locally and nationwide.

Dr. Beth currently lives in the Minneapolis area with her husband Michael Knotts. Together they produce "Recipes For Life with Dr. Beth" seen on local cable TV throughout MN, WI and NE.

Memberships: American Academy of Anti-aging, Omega Team and Resurrection Apostolic International Network (RAIN),

48 pages,

$4.95

120 pages,

$14.95

220 pages,
$19.95
Spiral
Bound
Cookbook!

64 pages,

$5.95

100 pages,

$9.95

120 pages,

$9.95

Also available by Dr. Beth

www.recipesforlifewithdrbeth.com

# of copies

TO PLACE AN ORDER:

___ ***Aspirin Alternatives: The Top Natural Pain-Relievers*** (Lombardi) $8.95
___ ***Bilberry & Lutein: The Vision Enhancers!*** (Ley) $4.95
___ ***Calcium: The Facts, Fossilized Coral*** (Ley) $4.95
___ ***Castor Oil: Its Healing Properties*** (Ley) $4.95
___ ***Dr. John Willard on Catalyst Altered Water*** (Ley) $5.95
___ ***Chlorella: Ultimate Green Food (Ley)*** $5.95
___ ***CoQ10: All-Around Nutrient for All-Around Health*** (Ley) $5.95
___ ***Coleus Forskohlii: Metabolic Modifier- Shape Up & Slim Down (Ley)*** *$4.95*
___ ***Colostrum: Nature's Gift to the Immune System*** (Ley) $5.95
___ ***Cordyceps: The Chinese Longevity Mushroom (Ley)*** *$4.95*
___ ***DHA: The Magnificent Marine Oil*** (Ley) $6.95
___ ***DHEA: Unlocking the Secrets/Fountain of Youth-2nd ed.*** (Ash & Ley)..........$14.95
___ ***Diabetes to Wholeness*** (Ley).......... $9.95
___ ***Discover the Beta Glucan Secret*** (Ley) $3.95
___ ***Dr. Beth's Weight Loss Solution*** (Ley) $9.95
___ ***Dr. Beth's Weight Loss Solution Kit*** (2 books, 4 dvds, ph test strips).......... $59.95
___ ***Fading: One family's journey ... Alzheimer's*** (Kraft)..........$12.95
___ ***Flax! Fabulous Flax!*** (Ley) $4.95
___ ***Flax Lignans: Fifty Years to Harvest*** (Sönju & Ley) $4.95
___ ***God Wants You Well*** (Ley) $14.95
___ ***How Did We Get So Fat? 2nd Edition*** (Susser & Ley) (SALE) $4.00
___ ***How to Fight Osteoporosis and Win!*** (Ley) $6.95
___ ***Iodine! (Ley)*** *$5.95*
___ ***Maca: Adaptogen and Hormone Balancer (Ley)*** $5.95
___ ***Medicinal Mushrooms:*** *Agaricus Blazei Murill (Ley)*..........$4.95
___ ***MSM: On Our Way Back to Health W/ Sulfur*** (Ley) SPANISH $3.95
___ ***MSM: On Our Way Back to Health W/ Sulfur*** (Ley) $4.95
___ ***Nature's Road to Recovery: Nutritional Supplements for the Alcoholic & Chemical Dependent*** (Ley) $5.95
___ ***pH: Optimal Health Through Alkaline Foods (Ley)***..........*$5.95*
___ ***PhytoNutrients: Medicinal Nutrients in Foods***, *Revised /Updated* (Ley) $5.95
___ ***Recipes For Life! (Spiral Bound Cookbook)*** (Ley)..........$19.95
___ ***Spewed! How to Cast Out Lukewarm Christianity through Fasting*** *(Ley)*. $15.95
___ ***Stress Epidemic: Adrenal Fatigue/Burnout*** (Ley/West)..........$14.95
___ ***The Potato Antioxidant: Alpha Lipoic Acid*** (Ley) $6.95
___ ***Vinpocetine: Revitalize Your Brain w/ Periwinkle Extract!*** (Ley) $5.95

Book subtotal $ __________ + $6.00 (U.S.) shipping = $____________

Send check or money order to: BL Publications 4851 Hausken Trail NE, Longville, MN 56655

Credit card orders please call toll free: 1-877-BOOKS11

Or visit: www.recipesforlifewithdrbeth.com